Draw CARTOONS

f folkes

ADAM & CHARLES BLACK · LONDON

First published 1982
Reprinted 1983
by A & C Black (Publishers) Ltd
35 Bedford Row, London WC1R 4JH

ISBN 0-7136-2197-4

Text set in VIP Palatino
Printed and bound in Great Britain
by J. W. Arrowsmith Ltd, Bristol

Contents

Making a start

Drawing cartoons can be either a hobby or a profession, to amuse your friends or try to make an editor laugh. The second is very difficult. The person you are most likely to amuse is yourself (which is very satisfying).

To be a cartoonist requires two simple things, neither of which are really simple. You have to think funny and you have to draw in a way that the reader can understand. The thinking funny is something that can't be taught, but this book may help you to get your ideas on paper.

It will be hard work as, unlike many other titles in this series which specialize in a particular subject such as cats, children or trees, you will have to learn to draw everything – possibly even including armadillos! (see page 40).

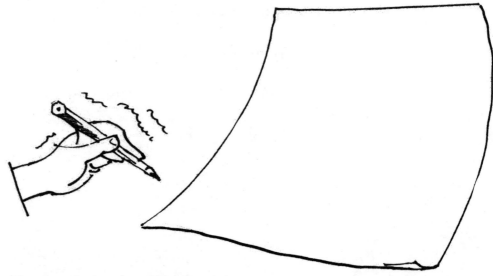

The dreaded piece of blank paper

4

A sketchbook is as necessary to the aspiring artist as was his mother's knee. Draw everything in sight – deckchairs (which are particularly tricky), watering cans, wheelbarrows, sofas, the cat – and keep your sketchbooks for future reference. It may be that none of these things will ever appear in a cartoon but you are training your hand and eye and the only way to learn how to draw is to draw as much and as often as possible (see next page).

Every object around you has its unique shape and colour and the more you know and can express about them the better.

Be as bold as you dare. It's your piece of paper, and you can do what you like with it. Experiment with the biggest piece of paper and the boldest, softest piece of chalk or crayon you can find, filling the paper with lines – scribbles, funny faces, lettering, anything – to get a feeling of freedom. Even if you think you have a gift for tiny delicate drawings with a fine pen or pencil, this is worth trying as a loosening-up exercise. The results may surprise you.

Quite often you will find a drawing isn't working out. Maybe the characters are in the wrong positions or on the wrong scale. Much better to scrap it and start again. If your second try is even worse, go and walk the dog or watch television and try again later.

Cartooning has to be fun. A lot of people will tell you that comic artists are very serious people and this, only too often, is true.

What to draw with

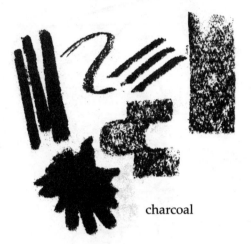

charcoal

charcoal pencil

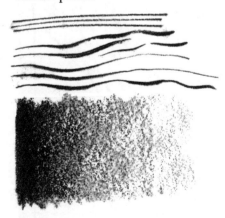

carbon pencil

pen and ink

To find the right materials to suit your drawing – paper, ink, nib etc. – takes time, just as the business of learning to draw takes time. It is a good idea to try several different media to find which you prefer.

Pencils are graded according to hardness, from 9H (the hardest, and only appropriate for stabbing yourself or your teacher to death) to H; then HB; then from B up to 6B (the softest). For most purposes, a soft pencil (HB or softer) is best. If you keep it sharp, it will draw as fine a line as a hard pencil but with less pressure, which makes it easier to control.

Charcoal (which is very soft) is excellent for large, bold sketches, but not for detail. If you use it, beware of accidental smudging. A drawing can even be dusted or rubbed off the paper altogether. To prevent this, spray with fixative. Charcoal pencils are also useful.

Wax crayons (also soft) are not easily smudged or erased. You can scrape a line away from a drawing on good quality paper, or partly scrape a drawing to get special effects.

Oil pastels, marker pencils, chinagraph and lithographic chalk are similar to wax crayons.

Conté crayons, wood-cased or in solid sticks, are available in various degrees of hardness, and in several colours. The cased crayons are easy to sharpen, but the solid sticks are more fun – you can use the side of the stick for large areas of tone. Conté is harder than charcoal, but it is also easy to smudge.

Pens vary as much as pencils or crayons. Ink has a quality of its own, but of course it cannot be erased. Nibs don't last very long. They soon become blunt and lose their delicacy and attractiveness.

Special artists' pens, such as Gillott 303 and Gillott 404 allow you a varied line, according to the angle at which you hold them and the pressure you use. The Gillot 659 is a very popular crowquill pen.

Reed, bamboo and quill pens are good for bold lines and you can make the nib end narrower or wider with the help of a sharp knife or razor blade. This kind of pen has to be dipped frequently into the ink.

brush handle dipped in ink

fibre pen – broad

fibre pen – fine

brush and paint

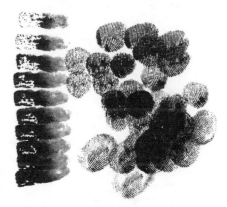

ink and finger

Fountain pens have a softer touch than dip-in pens, and many artists prefer them. The portability of the fountain pen makes it a very useful sketching tool.

Special fountain pens, such as Rapidograph and Rotring, control the flow of ink by means of a needle valve in a fine tube (the nib). Nibs are available in several grades of fineness and are interchangeable. The line they produce is of even thickness, but on coarse paper you can draw an interesting broken line similar to that of a crayon. These pens have to be held at a right-angle to the paper, which is a disadvantage.

Inks also vary. Waterproof Indian ink quickly clogs the pen. Pelikan Fount India, which is nearly as black, flows more smoothly and does not leave a varnishy deposit on the pen. Ordinary fountain-pen or writing inks (black, blue, green or brown) are less opaque, so give a drawing more variety of tone. You can mix water with any ink in order to make it thinner. But if you are using Indian ink, add distilled or rain water, because ordinary water will cause it to curdle.

Ball-point pens make a drawing look a bit mechanical, but they are cheap and fool-proof and useful for quick notes and scribbles.

Fibre pens are only slightly better, and their points tend to wear down quickly.

Brushes are very versatile drawing instruments. It is a strange thing, but a large brush that comes to a fine point can be as good for detail and retouching as a small one. You will discover which one suits you best.

Two things to remember: you can leave a pen to clean in a jug of water as long as you like – but never a brush, or it will quickly lose its shape.

There are plenty of other alternatives: Rembrandt was known to use his thumbnail with great effect.

What to draw on

A great variety of boards and papers is available in art shops. For the student a reasonably cheap but sturdy cartridge paper could be the answer. This has a slight roughness which is suitable for both pen and wash and, in fact, all the drawings in this book have been drawn on such a paper.

My own method is first to scribble out an idea in a sketchbook or on the back of an envelope, then rush it down on a sheet of detail paper and trace it on to paper or board?

A smooth surface is best for fine-line drawing. For watercolour it is preferable to work on a rougher texture (more 'tooth', as we say in the trade) as this type of paper is less absorbent and gives the artist more time to lay down a wash.

Many other materials are available, from cardboard to cigar boxes, but it may be wiser to use more conventional surfaces.

Line and watercolour

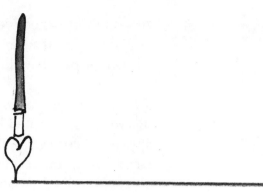

Line drawing requires a friendly pen or brush and a smooth piece of paper. Tones can be added not only by shading but also by a large variety of mechanical tints which you can cut out and apply yourself.

Watercolour or wash is a more complicated matter. The paper or board should have a rougher surface which, being less absorbent, will give you more time to control the brush and the flow of water and paint.

It is best to work fast; if washes are allowed to dry before the work is finished, hard lines will appear between one section of the drawing and another. For black and white drawings, I recommend Lamp Black. For colour, my own preference is for coloured inks which are brighter than watercolour and less likely to produce ugly joins. But then you have to work even faster!

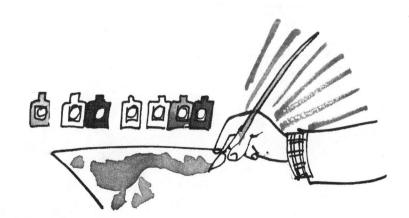

Perspective

Although perspective can be extremely complicated, it is not necessary for the cartoonist to know a lot about it. For us two vanishing points will do at the most, and one is often sufficient.

The role of perspective in drawing is to create a sense of depth or distance. All parallel horizontal lines that go away from you will appear to converge at the same vanishing point. If an object is facing you, only one vanishing point is required. When the object is moved to one side there will be two vanishing points.

Perspective lines can be drawn in lightly with a ruler and pencil. Don't forget to rub them out later.

Composition

To tell a story you have to use the right words. To draw a cartoon you have to use the right lines and sometimes (hopefully) the right words too.

Before you start on an idea, think how you will place it on the paper. Sometimes the composition will come into your mind at once but usually there are a few alternatives. The right one will make itself clear, given some thought. Try some rough sketches first.

Think of yourself as a cinema or theatrical director and compose your drawing with maximum dramatic effect. The scene you are about to set may be Mrs Hubbard finding the cupboard bare or a Babylonian feast – two very different subjects and challenges.

What you leave out is just as important as what you put in. Unnecessary detail that clutters up the basic idea should be avoided, however much you may wish to indulge yourself. The point of the cartoon should be as clear as possible.

Very bleak – they are starving

Haphazard wash to express pleasure

Essential lines

Here are some drawings that show how three very different characters can be developed from the same simple beginning.

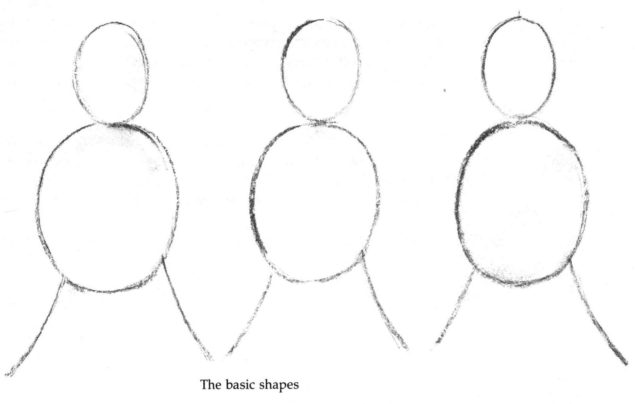

The basic shapes

Adding the first lines to convey expression and position

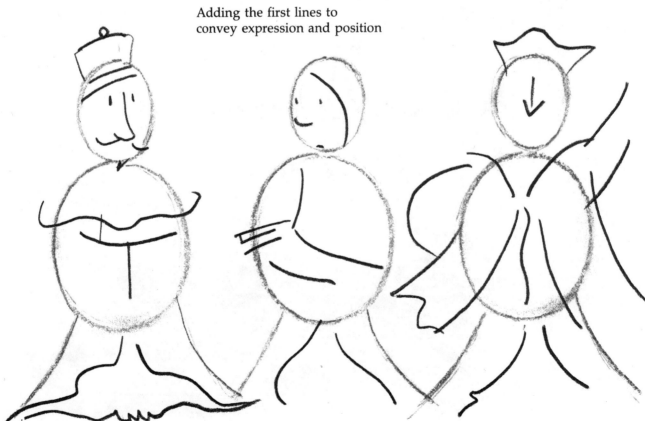

More detail

A few extras

The right proportions

People in cartoons aren't like real people in the street, they have different proportions; their heads are too big and their bodies too small. But once you get used to this, they may become more true to life than the real people.

They may look something like this at first . . .

. . . but perhaps they *really* look more like this.

As always, it is a good thing to have your sketchbook ready, but be discreet: some people hate to discover they are being drawn.

Paul Crum, a marvellous *Punch* cartoonist in the thirties, did a cartoon of two people looking at some penguins in the Zoo, with one saying, 'Why are some smaller than others?' I find this very funny, but don't ask me why. There is no answer to the question of why something amuses some people and not others.

Some being smaller than others may be the starting point for another cartoon.

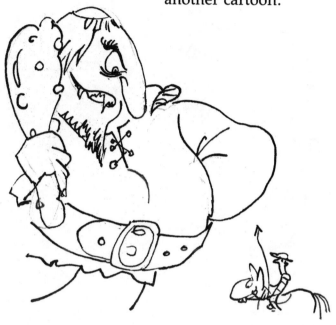

A drawing based on the idea that people are all the same small size and dwarfed by their surroundings.

The blot was a mistake. Maybe somebody exploded.

A cartoon step by step

I personally do not like to be confined to filling in in ink a prepared blueprint of a drawing but prefer to make it up as I go along. Here you must imagine me talking aloud as I work through the various stages of trying to create a cartoon.

It all starts with a scribbled caption on the back of an envelope.

Establish the central character

Increased baldness and give him spectacles. He becomes more vulnerable

Better position more tension

Fatter? Add stripes

Increase angle for dramatic effect and pose him dangerously on the edge

Start to fill in background detail

Subject – middle-aged business man *about* to throw himself off parapet.

Or has he *already* thrown himself off? No, it's more interesting to see what kind of man he is, rather than seeing only a pair of trouser-legs and shoes disappearing out of the picture.

Choose a dramatic angle to suggest height and a sense of danger.

as above

More action

Add final details like button-holes and skyscrapers.

"Miss Murdoch, he only wants a kiss."

Saying something personal

The essential thing about a cartoon is that it must say something personal to the reader about what has just gone on, what is going on, and what might go on – and, preferably, that it should take him by surprise.

Maybe you will have someone particular in mind when drawing a cartoon like this one . . .

'Sorry, sir, only vegetables.'

'He has a fine mind but he's
hopeless with his hands.'

To be a cartoonist is not like being an ordinary artist. You cannot just draw a pretty girl or a tree and leave it at that. You have to say something about them (even if there is no caption), and that is the difficult and intriguing part. What can you say about a tree? Think of Walt Disney's trees in *Snow White and the Seven Dwarfs*. Everything is possible.

All your best ideas will say something true about your own attitudes, however disguised they may be.

1   2

Simplicity and impact

The essence of a cartoon is that it is a story made understandable by a few strokes of the pen or brush. It should convey immediately who is talking to whom, why they are there and what is funny about the situation.

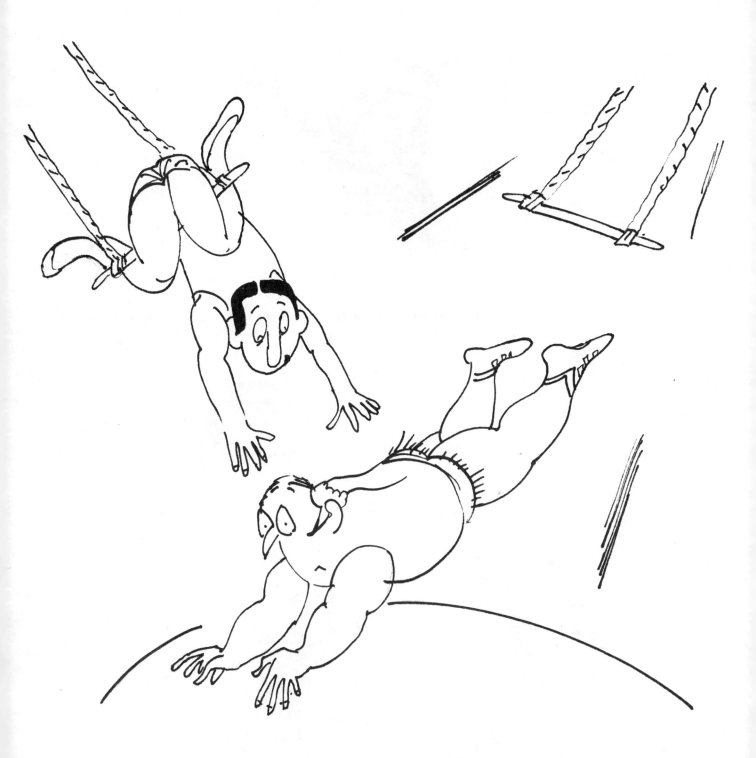

However complicated the drawing may become, the focus of attention must be on the original idea.

"Sorry, Charlie, nobody's perfect."

Variety

There are all sorts of things you can do in a cartoon. You can make fun of authority, be rude about your aunt, make animals speak, or rebuild Babylon.

The important thing is not to say or draw what has been done before but something new – even to you.

There are also infinite possibilities for variety in size and shape when drawing cartoons: some consist of a single drawing, some of a series of pictures running across the page; some are without words, others may have a great many words.

'The soup was thin, the steak was tough, the vegetables were over-done, the trifle was a mess and the wine probably corked. I happen to be a masochist so please reserve me a table for tomorrow.'

A personal card

To Edith
♥ George   on your birthday

'Of course I look smug. All skeletons look smug.'

'I can remember when this was an Adventure Playground.'

In the case of the strip cartoon, it is important to remember that there must be continuity from one drawing to the next. This requires discipline – it is best to work out the whole sequence before you start the final drawings.

'Think of the children!'

The shape of the picture can vary – according, perhaps, to the subject, or to the necessity for designing the drawing to fit into an already defined space (see also the next two pages).

As long as the cartoon is funny, it doesn't matter how it is presented.

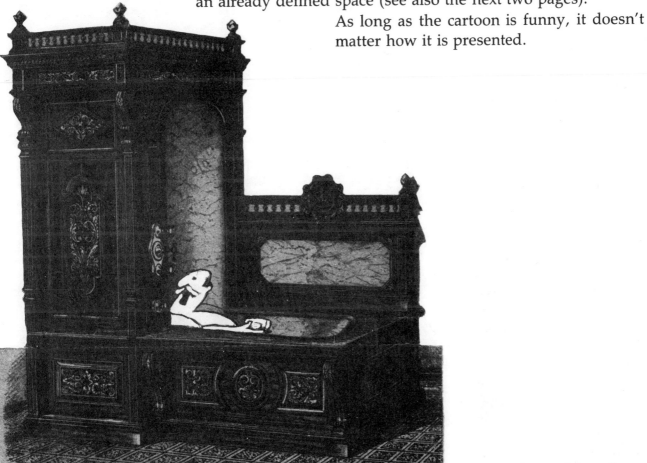

'Bedlington, this soap has woodworm.'

The pocket cartoon

'Fortunately I was refused the work-permit.'

The half-page cartoon

'Muriel, I am talking to you. Are you there?'

The full-page cartoon

A full-page drawing need not be elaborate but it must use the larger space in the most dramatic way. (See also pages 22–3.)

Part of the joke here is the difference in size of the tablets. Moses is already stooped under the weight.

'There's a P.S.'

Situations

One of the pleasures of a good cartoon is a sense of familiarity. We recognize as old friends the clubman in his armchair with his port or brandy, or the captain going down with his ship, giving the final salute. Here are some other situations which also contain familiar elements.

You must feel in your bones the time and place and make it as convincing as possible. An extra, telling detail can help a lot.

It is difficult to avoid the repetition of certain clichés. We have all seen too many desert island jokes, measles jokes and mother-in-law jokes. Such subjects represent the greatest challenge just because they have been done so many times before. But it is marvellous to think of a new variation.

Action

As in television, cinema or theatre, one of the most important ingredients of a cartoon is that things happen!

The pompous man slipping on a banana skin, the custard pie in the face of the dowager and the bull charging the picnic are three well-known and loved situations though now somewhat out of date. (Fashion changes in humour as in everything, so don't spend too much time looking at old cartoons – except for pleasure.)

Movement can be conveyed by an exaggerated gesture . . .

. . . or by a facial expression.

Greater momentum can be expressed by 'speed' lines.

Action is most effective in contrast to stillness. Here the violence of the farmer and the bull is accentuated by the serenity of the suburban gentleman with his carefully arranged picnic.

Provide your own caption.

Caricature

This is the ancient art of being rude on paper. Everything can be caricatured, but here we are concerned with the human face.

It is really a question of exaggerating the more obvious characteristics.

Sort of Etruscan

Rather mediaeval

Kind of renaissance

Distinctly Victorian

W. E. GLADSTONE

Of course, the mouth could have been drawn in, but it seemed unnecessary. The slight blot under the nose was an accident, but accidents can suggest unexpected ideas.

Two different characters. Look carefully for the more obvious features, strengths and weaknesses that characterize your subject – eyebrows, nose, jaw line, hair or lack of it.

By increasing the length of a nose or diminishing a chin you may probably lose all your friends.

The profile is the easiest form of caricature so the most tempting to try, but let the person's face dictate what you should do.

Some faces may suggest a full frontal attack.

A true likeness

The previous four pages dealt exclusively with the face, but a likeness is not only conveyed by a head on a pair of shoulders. Everyone has a different way of crossing his legs, holding a glass or rubbing his nose. Here is someone doing all three at the same time.

Even the armchair he is sitting in has its own character.

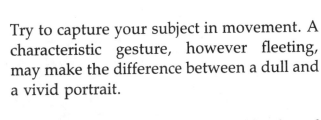

Try to capture your subject in movement. A characteristic gesture, however fleeting, may make the difference between a dull and a vivid portrait.

Here it is helpful to use a sketchbook and take a number of quick notes, committing as much as you can to memory. When you come to making the finished drawing, choose from both what makes the best likeness.

Tooth and claw

One of the largest populations in the cartoon world is that of the animal kingdom. The curious thing about these creatures is that they all speak excellent English.

A visit to the Zoo would be a good idea here. The movement and colour of live animals are an important part of their essential characteristics and are far more exciting than a print or photograph can convey.

Try, always, to capture the unique quality of these individuals –
for individuals they are. Penguins look as though they might fly
but don't. Swans look as if they can't fly, but do.

To my mind, drawing a duckbill platypus is more amusing than
drawing a traffic warden. (On second thoughts there may not be
much difference.)

Another great pleasure in drawing animal cartoons is the variety of patterns and textures you can employ. Here is a selection.

But of course there are lots more.

Different subjects, different media

To enjoy drawing, it is valuable to develop as many skills as possible, and to be able to control a pen without making too many blots and a brush without too many splashes.

The subject may dictate which medium is to be used. If your aim is to produce an Oriental style, it must be the brush.

'Your pagoda or mine?'

For recreating a typical nine-teenth-century effect which will require plenty of crosshatching, a fine pen which can manage the thicks and thins would be a good solution.

'Do you love me or don't you?'

Charcoal and wash give a sense of spontaneity to this light-hearted idea.

'Darling, I think you brood too much.'

Finished works

One of the more curious things about life, among men anyway, is that so many seem to want to be cartoonists. If only they knew!

The truth is that it is a life-long pursuit of the occasional golden glow, showered by rejection slips.

So let us suppose that you intend to draw not just for your own amazement but for publication in a newspaper or magazine.

You may prefer to add tone to a line drawing to make greater impact. These methods have been discussed earlier in the book but one other way to obtain a mechanical tint is to apply a light blue wash where the tint is required (this does not photograph) and ask the printer to add the tint to these areas.

When presenting your work it should be as neat and uniform as possible (cut roughs to the same size) and should include at least one finished drawing to demonstrate your skill. On no account explain the jokes in your letter; and send a stamped addressed envelope for their return. Pack the work with a piece of cardboard or your carefully created cartoons may come back looking like a bag of crisps.

The use of colour for reproduction is rather a luxury but will reproduce in black and white if necessary.

Remove all errors with as little visible effort as possible. Someone, friend or editor, may wish to hang your drawing on the wall or publish it in his paper.

It should look like an act of God.

47

Envoi

Cartooning can be a very pleasant way of spending time, both in dreaming up ideas and in putting them down on paper. It gives you the opportunity of saying a few rude things about what *you* have to put up with – your family, school or job, for example.

I hope this book may have helped you to express your own point of view, to look around you a little harder, and perhaps eventually to increase your bank balance.

Everyone needs to be entertained and some people even have a sense of humour. Hopefully, yours.